AUTHENTICALLY ME

Authentically Me

THE ESSENCE OF GOD

B.E. Felder

Bobby Felder II, Editor

Soul 7 Publishing

Authentically Me:
The Essence of God

———————————————

B.E. Felder

Authentically Me: The Essence of God

Copyright © 2021 by B.E. Felder

All rights reserved. No part of this book may be reproduced or transmitted in any form or by any means without written permission from the author.

ISBN 9780578729060

Printed in USA by

Dedication

To my wife and the love of my life of 43 years, Georgina Lynn McCain Felder. She has been a rock throughout this entire process.

To my mother, the late Alberta Felder Jackson, the motivation and inspiration of my life. She always made me feel special, and most of all she believed in me. She encouraged me to live life without regrets. I love you mother.

Contents

Dedication	vii
part	xi
Preface	xiii
Introduction	xv
I THE AUTHENTIC AND THE UNAUTHENTIC	1
II IDENTIFYING: THE PHYSICAL AND NON- PHYSICAL EXISTENCE	12
III AWAKENING: DISCOVERING CONSCIOUSNESS AND AWARENESS	21
IV THE AUTHENTICALLY RESPONSIBLE SELF: THE GIFT OF CHOICE	30
V TRUE RESPECT, REVERENCE AND UNITY	37
VI BREAKING THE CYCLE OF ILLUSION: LIVING IN THE NEWLY DISCOVERED CYCLE OF TRUTH	46

VII	THE TRUTH	53
VIII	BECOMING AUTHENTICALLY ME: "THE PRACTITIONER"	63
IX	AUTHENTICALLY ME	77

Acknowledgements   83

Preface

This book is an exposition of my personal journey of discovering and identifying my true self. This journey has been amazing, eye opening and continues to bring new and exhilarating aspects of enlightenment and freedom to my life. As I have discovered the absolute truth of who I am, I have an overwhelming and vigorous desire to share this awakening phenomenon with others. This is not an autobiography or memoir, rather it is an articulation of a moment in time necessary for me to discover a missing interval within my life as I have lived it thus far. The words and events inked throughout the chapters of this book will serve as a means for me to share part of my experiences on this journey of light.

My prayer is that those who will read this book will launch within themselves to find their true and authentic person and enter a wonderful life of freedom and liberty.

Introduction

I am a minister and teacher, and my commitment to the work of ministry has extended over more than forty years. In the past four decades, I have been helping others by ministering and teaching them through love, compassion, and empathy. Through caring for and attending to others, I have seen many people change their lives and truly become different right before my eyes. I have seen the depressed and suicidal regain hope. I have seen the addict of decades choose to no longer live the same existence. I have seen broken marriages, families and relationships mended and restored, weight and strength returned to ailing bodies and life restored. However, through all the years of working in ministry, there was an ultimate feeling of fulfillment that was absent.

I asked myself, what is it? What am I missing? Why do I still have a void in my life, especially seemingly having experienced some of the greatest moments of other individuals' lives? These were questions that troubled and plagued my mind through thoughts of nonfulfillment and vacancy. It was at this time of questioning that I would begin my quest to locate the missing piece and fill the empty space in the puzzle that was in my life. In this journey, I did not want to view anything through a smoke screen. I did not want to have to interpret what I was hearing, seeing, or feeling about myself. What I desired and sought out was the pure, unadulterated, naked, and perhaps even harsh truth. Only this kind of truth to me could and would ultimately make me complete.

My discovery would be one that I could never have imagined! As aforesaid, it continues to perpetually enlighten and empower my life. Along my journey of discovering who I was, I had to ask myself some questions. In the quest for the answers to those questions, I discovered the true and authentic person that I am. The true me: AUTHENTICALLY ME!

In the chapters to follow we will identify the dual identities, as well as spheres of existence we experience in life. This awareness will help us to better understand many struggles we have within ourselves (feelings, emotions, so called character flaws). This will be the genesis of delving into our discovery of consciousness and truth, as well as the responsibility of accepting it as such. In accepting and walking in this new consciousness and truth, we will discuss and get a new understanding of true respect and reverence. We will learn how to break the cycle of illusion and live in the newly discovered cycle of truth. Ultimately, you will be able to identify your authentic self and live the remainder of your existence knowing who you really are.

I

THE AUTHENTIC AND THE UNAUTHENTIC

"Authentically Me" is derived from the words true [authentic] and self [me]. Merriam Webster's dictionary describes authentic as being real or genuine, not a copy. The full definition of authentic is inclusive of originality, in that it is true to one's personality, spirit and character. There is no imitation or fakeness in the picture; it is clearly authentic. In this search for my authentic self, I wanted that pure truth. Consequently, every moment had to be the truth and nothing but the truth, and I was truly ready and willing to look into the mirror of my truth.

The word me or self describes who a person or someone is naturally and unimpededly. It is reflective of what makes one person different from another even in the combinations of emotions, thoughts, feelings, etc. It is the entire person of an individual, and the realization or embodiment of one's natural character or behavior. This search was about the true me; my emotions, thoughts, feelings, and all the realization of who I really and truly am.

> *To know our authentic self, we will experience the 'Turbulence Expedition"*

Imagine flying on a plane and the pilot announces the height in which the plane will be flying. However, to get there, he announces that we will experience a few minutes of turbulence. It is at this moment you realize that turbulence becomes the mediation for the peace that is above the clouds. Once you are above the clouds there are no storms, and therefore, no need for resistance. That moment of turbulence is welcomed once we realize the peace that rests on the other side. To know the authentic self, we will experience the "Turbulence Expedition". When we are on a genuine quest for truth, it can always be found within ourselves. Though we may experience a little turbulence along the way, we must realize that it is only a seemingly aggressive distraction before the clear and redefining (truth) moment is revealed.

The mirror is only a reflection of the authentic you.
It is not who you truly are.

When you look into a mirror, the image in the mirror is not you, although it is a physical image or representation of you. You may look in the mirror and sometimes notice little flaws on the outer surface that you can fix. However, as you look in the mirror, you cannot physically see what is behind the image in that reflection. The mirror merely reflects the form of the authentic you. It is not who you are.

The mirror cannot present or reflect presence or being, only the reflection of an illusion which can be manipulated to look any way you wish. What most people see in the mirror is who they think they are, and consequently, they try to live like the individual they see in the mirror should live. The reality is that they are living their life in and from an (unauthentic) illusion instead of experiencing and living from the authentic self. You must always remember that to access your true self, you will have to go beyond the mirror, beyond the veil, beyond the flesh.

It is important to understand that for everything authentic, there exist an unauthentic version or imitation of it. There is an authentic and unauthentic God, world, truth, self, Christ, personality, hell, heaven, gospel, marriage, family, worship, witness, body, report, love, salvation, hope, image, gift, prophecy, vision, intuition, prayer, power, respect. There are authentic and unauthentic teachers, feelings, angels, demons, prophets, and the list goes on and on and on. In other words, etc. Once we realize and really pay attention to this reality, we arrive at the entrance of awareness (consciousness).

Jesus asked his followers two questions concerning his identity. The first question was, "who do *they* (the general population) say that I am?" And the second question to the disciples was, who do *you* say that I am?

> *Matthew 16:13-16*
> *¹³ When Jesus came into the coasts of Caesarea Philippi, he asked his disciples, saying,*
> *Whom do men say that I the Son of man am?*
> *¹⁴ And they said, Some say that thou art John the Baptist: some, Elias; and others, Jeremias, or one of the prophets.*
> *¹⁵ He saith unto them, But whom say ye that I am?*
> *¹⁶ And Simon Peter answered and said, Thou art the Christ, the Son of the living God.*
> *-KJV*

During this time on earth, Jesus stood out. His discovery of who he was made him different from most. There were kings, priests, and noble men during those times. However, the message Jesus spoke and lived is what caused his death. He knew who he was and the power he had. The general population looked at him as a mystical being. However, he wanted to know from the disciples what their view was, especially being so close to him. It was Peter who looked beyond the veil and spoke the confirmation of who Jesus really was.

Let us look at three ways a person can view or look at themselves. The first way is how the world or general population views them. The second way is the way those who are in their inner circle view them. Lastly, is the way they view or look themselves. Even though Jesus asked those questions, He was sure of His own identity. Jesus then identified himself to them as the Son of God.

The world will judge your outer surface, your vocation, position, financial status, even your culture. Your associates and relatives will judge your thoughts, emotions, and behavior. While others may claim to know you or give their opinion of who you are, you must "KNOW" who you truly are. Your intuition will know your authentic self; the self that God knows, reflects upon and bear's witness to. Not only do we need to know who we are, we need to experience who we are.

> *Inner Strength is Obtained by the Affirmation of our Authentic Self*

Most people do not live in and from the authentic self, rather they live the unauthentic version of their true reality. I cannot characterize this using percentages, numbers, or specific data; however, it can be characterized by the way the general population is consistently seeking its personal identity through external validation.

Nowadays it is so important for people to be validated and identified from the outside, that they never think to search the place that the true validation should come from. No one really knows your thoughts, your feelings, your motives, or intent. All they see and know is how you are presented or appear to them. When you base your identity on validation that comes from someone else, that perception is their authentic perception, not your authentic reality.

When one lives an unauthentic existence, it is hard for them to identify and clearly see their true purpose and potential in this life. They constantly find themselves unhappy with who they are, where they are, and their supposition of where they are going in this life. This happens because their true purpose has been distorted by their tainted personal view of themselves. This twisted and distorted view is caused by being identified from external validation rather than from internal light. You do not need external validation to be authentic.

While being affirmed or validated by others is not necessarily a bad thing, it often helps aid people with self-esteem and confidence issues. However, it is that inner strength that is obtained by affirmation of our authentic self that validates us. Many people are told who they are by others. For that cause, many people's personal view of themselves is the perception of how others view them. Consequently, they are acting out a life never examining the true identity of themselves, but rather they are living their lives by the opinion, view, or words of others. This is the unauthentic self. When we fail to realize our true existence, we live our lives never being fully present, just existing. We must learn to appreciate who we are and be fulfilled even when others do not.

One of my favorite stories told to me as a toddler was about a younger train being encouraged by an elder train to never give up. The young train would affirm itself and say "I think I can, I think I can" over and over. That little train declared that statement until it believed it could do it. The ending result for the train was mission accomplished. The power was inside of the train, and once the young train discovered that even though encouragement came from the outside (from elder train), the power was within the train itself.

AFFIRM OUR POTENTIAL INTO REALITY

When I was in high school, I played basketball on a team that had a history of winning. I was one of the five starters on the varsity team. The school (Snook High School) was recognized for winning many state basketball championships within its district. There was always a star player on the team that shined above the rest. Even though there were other good players and teammates, there was always one player who was considered the star of the game. However, when it came to winning, everyone shined after the game was over.

I recall leading up to one game, that the captain of the team would be unable to play due to illness. He was usually the star player of the game. The coach asked if I would fill in for him. His position was point guard, as well as captain. My usual position was forward. This player was a phenomenal player. As I aforementioned, he was often the star player of the game. My confidence was extremely low filling in as the captain and switching position from forward to point guard. This was like occupying a dual leadership position that was frightening to me. I looked up to the captain player so much that I never even remotely imagined myself in his shoes.

The coach noticed that I had low confidence and begin to speak with and encourage me. He told me I was the purist shooter on the team. I just did not know it. He told me we were going to practice on a play that was designed just for me before the next game. His encouragement was uplifting, but I had to gain confidence that I could fill the role. I just told myself over and over, "I can do it". Long story short, we won the game, and I scored a lot of points. I was the star of the game. From that point on, whether I was the star player or not, I never doubted my abilities on the court again.

We must learn to affirm our potential into reality. While we have encouragement from others, we must have that authentic faith to believe in ourselves as the catalyst for change. The young train accomplished its mission through affirmation of itself, just as I affirmed my ability to be a star player. Affirmations are used to bring into evidence what is not yet manifested. David's Psalms 23 is a prime example of an affirmation, of his quest for his authentic self and the universal theme of our trust and faith in God.

In the glass of transparency, all colors come from one light

Growing up in school, we learned about the prism of colors. During this learning process, we discovered that all colors were projected by and through the glass of transparency. In the glass of transparency, all colors come from one light. While we see many colors and a beautiful and perfect diamond, the truth is that they all come from the white light shining by and through them. There is only one authentic you. Many characteristics and personality traits, but only one true you. In the scriptures Jesus asked the disciples who He was. The disciples responded by describing the many traits or characteristics of who He was, and even though Jesus possessed all those characteristics, He knew His true and authentic being. Bottom line, know who you are.

As an artist, I can paint a picture so real that after I finish it, I can escape right into it. When I look at it, I see something I have captured on canvas, yet, I can also go into the theme anytime I have a desire to. How? All I have to do is look at it and escape. When I get inside the painting, I see everything that I created. I can even see myself inside the painting. I see the creator and the creation. The premise of this is that there are many characteristics within the painting, but they all come from one creator. We must be authentic and transparent with ourselves. Learn to see yourself inside of you.

When we discover the diamond of our authentic self, it should be a learning experience and not an ignorant one. The power of authenticity lies within us. According to scripture, **Genesis 1:26-28** quotes:

> *₂₆ Then God said, Let us make man in our image, according to our likeness; let them have dominion*
> *over the fish of the sea, over the birds of the air, and over the cattle, over all the earth and*
> *over every creeping thing that creeps on the earth.*
> *₂₇ So God created man in his own image, in the image of God He created him; male and female*
> *created He created them.*
> *₂₈ Then God blessed them, and God said to them, Be fruitful and multiply; till the earth and subdue it;*
> *have dominion over the fish of the sea, over the birds of the air, and over every*
> *living thing that moves on the earth.*
> *-KJV*

We were made in and of the essence of God. Wow! And we were given the gift of responsibility and choice that came with the authority (dominion) to use as we wish. With all, one question remains. Why do so many still live an unauthentic existence or never come to the realization of who they are? The answer is simple. So many people still believe their non-authentic self is in fact their authentic self.

Throughout the rest of this journey, my goal is to share with you how I and you can dismantle the veil that is the unauthentic self by exposing "*the illusion*". This discovery will lead to the road of becoming authentically me. There is an old adage that says, you cannot help someone else if you cannot help yourself. With that being said, you have to know who you are in order to help yourself, and then you can proceed to help others. Taking the expedition of exploring the person within will help you to attain that authenticity of who you really are. The one that not only knows itself but can help others along the way.

II

IDENTIFYING: THE PHYSICAL AND NON-PHYSICAL EXISTENCE

It is beyond the veil that our genesis and our most heartfelt values are kept.

The physical (visible) existence (world) is our human nature with content (flesh), which is perceived by our five senses and visible makeup. Our non-physical (invisible) existence (world) is our Being, which is without form or content and cannot be perceived by our five senses. Yet, our physical existence is conscious of the non-physical existence through our subconscious or intuition. The framework of this phenomenon is called "The Human-Being". This is the make-up of every individual. We are flesh and blood, however there is a part of us that is not visible to the naked eye that is called our "Being".

It is in this invisible (non-physical) world that our origins and our most heartfelt values are stored (retained). They become explicable and incomprehensible to a degree in which the five senses alone cannot perceive. Our authentic Being aligns with the compelling nature of our authentic self. Our Being allows our content (human) to recognize, through its non-content (spirit), that we are filled with meaning, purpose, and inspiration (*enthusiasm*); that life is love with no thoughts or fear. This all while our human side aligns with our five senses, only perceiving the physical world and its concepts. It is our Being that connects us to the non-physical world or spirit.

Please do not misunderstand what is being said concerning the five senses, as they are not bad or negative. The senses are a part of our human faculties that allow us to see, smell, taste, hear, and touch, while our Being takes us beyond human content. According to **1 Corinthians 2:14,** the human side simply cannot comprehend the nonphysical reality, and it never was intended to.

"The natural cannot perceive the things of the spirit"
-KJV

Imagine living your life with two worlds before you. One world is the physical existence of mind, identification, and physical form. The other world is non-physical and has no identification or physical form. You have access to both worlds inside and outside (Human-Being) because you are the medium. The realization of this metaphor is that we live in both worlds simultaneously, but we must use more than our five senses to access the non-physical world. In other words, we must go beyond the veil or flesh.

> *Our physical existence was created and is sustained by our non-physical existence.*

To use only the five senses of our capability, we as a species and as individuals will never be free of pain, anxiety, depression, violence, and destruction. By only using our five senses or content, self can never fully appreciate and take advantage of the part that our physical existence plays in the nonphysical realm. Our physical existence was created and is sustained by our non-physical existence [*world*]. **Hebrews 11:3** quotes:

> *"By faith we understand that the worlds were framed by the word of God, so that the things which are seen were not made of things which are visible."*
>
> *-KJV*

Spending Time in the "Bubble of Faith"

I'm certain that many of you remember playing cowboys and Indians growing up. I was a junior in high school and still loved playing cowboys and Indians. We lived in the country, so this was brilliant amusement. My brother, who was a couple of years younger, and I would play cowboys and Indians with this old gun we had found around the house. It was a real gun, but it was incredibly old. We did not see any bullets in it, and it became one of our "toys" as we dubbed it to use during our adventures.

On one Sunday morning, I was washing my hands in the bathroom sink as the family and I were preparing to go to church. Suddenly, I heard a loud gun shot. I turned around and saw my little brother lowering the old gun in my direction. It was not until then that I discovered I had been shot. Again, we lived in the country about 20-25 minutes from the nearest hospital, so it's not difficult to imagine the anxiety driven activity going on at that time. My family put me in the vehicle and started to town. While in the vehicle, I remember myself *being* in a bubble of calmness. Everyone around me was hysterical, but I was calm.

As we made it through the emergency room entrance, the medical staff immediately started to work on me. They conducted an x-ray which reveals to them the entrance, as well as the exit of the bullet. It had pierced in and pierced out. The x-rays also showed that the bullet had narrowly missed my spine. My treatment was a womb dressing wrapped around my torso, and I was sent home the same day, all while spending time in the bubble of faith. My bubble allowed me to be whole. It was the gap between my physical and my non-physical self. I went behind the veil and experienced "Being". I knew I was and would be okay, even before I was ever examined.

There were times that I would take moments inside of that bubble long before the day I was shot. I would go in the woods and detach myself from anything negative and just relax my mind, having no thoughts. I would just enjoy myself without a name or physical existence. When I was shot, my mind went to that same place of non-physical existence. Because I could escape the present circumstance by going inside the bubble, I was able to navigate through that experience without any physical and emotional pain.

My brother was in a much more devastated mental and emotional space. Fortunately, seeing and knowing that I was mentally and physically sound and well, aided in his healing process. That bubble of faith experience would be an experience that I still cherish and use to this very day. It takes you beyond your physical existence and places you on the other side of you. It is a place of freedom and liberty beyond your imagination.
Matthew 6:6 says:

"But thou, when thou prayest, enter into thy closet, and when thou hast shut thy door, pray to thy Father which is in secret; and thy Father which seeth in secret shall reward thee openly."
KJV

Before you and I were made physical and had a personality, we were a nonphysical being. **Jeremiah 1:5** quotes:
"Before I formed you in the womb, I knew you;
Before you were born, I sanctified you; and ordained
(positioned) you.
-KJV

This passage in Jeremiah is expression from a person who was very much in touch with his nonphysical existence. Jeremiah is one with his Being, his authentic self (extension of God). The soul is a part of the nonphysical world and is eternal just as God. The universal soul is eternal. This Being Jeremiah spoke of existed before he was created. Every person has a Being, and that part of them is eternal; it will never die. Jeremiah was speaking of the non-physical world that existed long before he was born or even conceived in his mother's womb. The world without form, mind or identification. Most people live within their sensory personalities and never enter the awareness of their Being, their authentic self (beyond physical existence).

> **The challenge you and I face is becoming aware of our nonphysical self (Being) or "Essence of God".**

Understanding these sayings is easier said than done, because the five senses cannot discern the soul. The five sensory self can only discern our personality. The challenge you and I face is becoming aware of our nonphysical self [Being] or "Essence of God". The only way to become totally awakened to the revelation of our authentic self is to transcend our five sensory selves, our religiosity and external spirituality. We must look through the veils of mystery to find the truth about who we authentically are. Take love for instance.

> **Love is the connection between the physical and nonphysical world**

Love is the unifying source of the universe. Love connects the physical and non-physical world. Imagine using your physical lungs, muscles, esophagus, tongue, and lips to whistle or say, "I love you". The whistle is the wind and is created by the content of our body, but the wind of the whistle it not visible, nor are the words, "I love you". The lungs, muscles, esophagus, tongue, and lips are the only things visible. Our inhale and exhale allow physical life, which we visibly see in the flesh, but we cannot see life as spirit, yet we feel its flow. Our physical existence is our proof that life (God) exists on earth. However, the breath of life is non-physical and rest in our Being. The evidence is that we are alive. We are breathing, and though we cannot literally see the breath of life, we see what the breath displays or demonstrates in the physical, and its existence is us.

Prior to my grandmother's transition from her earthly journey, I had little understanding of death. I was too young to really comprehend what was going on. When she died, my mind did not know how to let her go physically. I was always looking for her to walk into the room, cook dinner, clean the house, or just hear her voice. She was such a loving person with a strong family bond of love and happiness. Even though everyone was saying she is gone to heaven and not coming back, it was simply not registering with me. I knew I had to come to grips somehow in my mind and accept that she is really gone and not coming back.

I remember building a medium to her in my mind; a place for her to exist. It was so strong that my subconscious would present her to me in my dreams. This was my way to keep a connection with her. I realized that my conscious mind had created that medium for the strength and love that she had given, which I needed to regain my strength after her passing. As I got older and grew stronger, the dreams and appearances grew less and less and eventually stopped. However, I could still communicate with her through the lasting memories of her love, strength and physical presence.

Later in life, I told my mother of how I got over my grandmother's death and the dreams that I would have of her. My mother told me that the same exact thing happened to her. My mother was the oldest child of my grandmother, and I was the oldest grandchild. My mother was a matriarch just as my grandmother was. She had that bond of love and vibrancy. She was strong and a leader in the family. When my mother passed away in 2015, I had a better understanding of death, though I still experienced the same thing as when I was a child. The only difference was that I was much older with my mother's death. One of the most enlightening take-aways from these experiences is that love will always transcend death.

III

AWAKENING: DISCOVERING CONSCIOUSNESS AND AWARENESS

What is consciousness? Consciousness is the state of awareness that happens without thought and form. Consciousness does not think, because it is beyond thought (content); consciousness is our innate awareness. This awareness is that mental impression, that inkling that moves through our subconscious senses from within our consciousness, which is beyond the mind or thought. It requires no effort. In fact, when we use thought and form to try and understand consciousness, we miss awareness and take ourselves into mere carnality. It has been referred to by other conscious individuals as the "third eye" or "sixth sense". This is where we need to surrender our content self and its faculties to our non-content Being. This is actually surrendering to God.

The part of you known as *"Being"* is the essence of the inner, the within. Being is *PRESENCE beyond human existence.* Presence is the essence, which is to know your Being as nature to you. This is the God within, the *authentic you* that you are becoming enlightened to. You come to realize the Presence or the Essence of who you are. You also realize that this part of you has no content, no flesh. It is your heart (center) and spirit, the make-up of your existence.

Through this, you come to know the power of acceptance. You receive and welcome the reality of your authentic self, which can sometimes be difficult to accept and embrace. I do realize that this read contains information that is a bit much to ingest and digest, especially when we've been so used to living from and navigating our lives with our minds, thoughts, feelings and content. I can concede that waking up and realizing consciousness was somewhat petrifying for me, because I was so accustomed to the outer experience of who I was. However, waking up to the realization that I was living someone else's life was far more terrifying.

To become aware, conscious or awakened is not a revelation of who you are, it is in fact who you are. It is *Be*ing. Please understand the difference between this consciousness and the mind, or ability to think. Your mind is your tool used for practical use and purposes. It has thoughts, emotions, innovations, a memory of your past and the projection of your future. However, the mind is not your consciousness. Your consciousness is beyond your mind. It simply IS. It is your "I AM". Whenever you choose, you can escape your mind and experience consciousness without effort, because it is what it is and who you are. You are consciousness, the Essence of Presence.

The Flower has consciousness without having to think

Imagine being a beautiful flower in bloom. It uses no effort to be beautiful or bloom. It just is and blooms without the worry (thought) of trying to make itself do so. Think of yourself as the flower. You do not have to use effort to *be* who you are; you are completely who you are with absolutely no effort. The flower has consciousness without having to think. The same applies to your consciousness. It exists without thinking.

Acts 17: 27-28 says:

²⁷ That they should seek the Lord, if haply they might feel after him, and find him, though he be not far from every one of us:
²⁸ For in him we live, and move, and have our being; as certain also of your own poets have said, for we are also his offspring.
-KJV

This scripture identifies the search and discovery of our human existence and our awakened to Being. We read concerning after this human existence is over in **II *Corinthians 5:1***

For we know that if our earthly house of this tabernacle were dissolved, we have a building of God, a house not made with hands, eternal in the heavens.
-KJV

In this scripture we realize the awareness and truth of our authentic self. We are both human and Being, otherwise known as Human-Being. We will exist in human nature for an appointed time. After that journey is over, we will exit this human flesh and continue on as our eternal Being.

Do not become a prisoner of your own mind

The most common mistake of our society is to think that we are our minds, and therefore locking ourselves into thought patterns of bondage. Do not become a prisoner of your own mind! I can hear you posing the question now. How can you become locked in the prison of your mind? How can your mind become a prison? The answer: All of your thoughts, emotions, pain, suffering, past, and projected future are in your mind. Your mind is the matrix or the grid of your reality. Whether it be positive or negative, it is still in your mind. When you cannot escape the negative forces of your mind, it then becomes a prison to you. Your mind is in bondage and needs a way of escape.

The mind is needed and is used as a practical tool or resource in the human existence we know as life. It does not identify our true self, but rather mirrors our identity. It is then that it can easily become a prison. You are locked inside the bars that surround it and cannot get out because you keep waiting for someone or something outside to unlock the door. You must realize that you have power over your mind and that it serves you; that you cannot be imprisoned by something that you rule.

The question now becomes: How do we escape our mind? Escaping your mind will first require a mere desire to do so. Somehow, YOU must get on the other side of it without waiting on something or someone to unlock the door. Free yourself! We must do as our spiritual ancestors and masters taught us. We must go to the inside and escape within, finding the keys to unlock our prisons. The art of meditation and prayer are good ways to escape your human existence into your presence. This technique requires us to have an acceptance of self, a non-resistance to self, and to BE self. Your purity is who you are. It is not your past or future life. *It* is who you are, NOW. **I Corinthians 2:9** quotes:

⁹ But as it is written, Eye hath not seen, nor ear heard, neither have entered the heart of man, the things which God hath prepared for them that love him.
-KJV

Living in the moment is your future

Your future becomes your now as each day progresses. It is called "living in the moment". Tomorrow becomes your today, today is your now, your now is your moment. Live each day in the moment. The future, when you try to live in it today, is an illusion [mind position]. When you live in the past and the future, you dishonor and overlook the present. Therefore, most people miss out on life because they live in what happened yesterday and wait for tomorrow to bring them something positioned and mirrored in their mind. Your true power is in your now, which is consciousness. Nothing can be more real and more powerful than your consciousness, or your awareness of NOW! The future will become now, as the past was now when it happened. Nothing truly exists but the moment. This knowledge alone will get you on the right path to consciousness. Learn to appreciate and live in the moment (Now). Remember, do not become a prisoner of your mind, but rather position your mind to awaken to consciousness.

The mind allows us to know who we truly are through the dynamic of consciousness.

To become conscious or have an awakened experience can be very enlightening. It is presence. It is God. Discovering Awareness and Consciousness is simultaneously a humbling experience, and it is one of the most powerful experiences you can ever have. The experience is humbling because you come to realize, know, and become your authentic self. Please again, understand and keep in mind that our minds are the most powerful tools we can use for practical life purposes. The mind is our guide to life's journey through its subconscious response to our consciousness. The mind allows us to know who we truly are through the dynamic of consciousness. Presence and Essence is who we authentically are.

I remember my first day of school when I was five years old. I can vividly remember the shirt, pants, socks, and the shoes I wore. It was the first day and year I started school. Each year, I grew and had to have new clothes and shoes. Just as I grew physically, so did my intellect. However, there was something about me that never changed. It was my presence and essence. When I turned fifty years old, I realized that I had the same presence and essence as the day I started school at five years old. This is when I began to truly experience and become aware of the authentic true self (ME).

> *When we are conscious of who we are, we are awakened to the consciousness of humanity within us*

Do not be afraid to know and experience your true self. When we are conscious of who we truly are, we are awakened to the consciousness of humanity within us. The only person that knows you are conscious is you. When you go beyond the simple mind, the awareness parallel lines begin to connect in you. The parallel lines then become one. That line is you and your moment; your NOW. This phenomenon happens in everyone's life, whether consciously or unconsciously.

> *I Corinthians 1:27*
> *To whom God would make known what is the riches of the glory of this mystery among the Gentiles;*
> *which is Christ in you, the hope of glory:*
> *-KJV*

Discovering consciousness is the most exciting thing that can happen to a person, because they are discovering themselves that they never knew. Just image introducing yourself to yourself and discovering it was God! Woah! That is Consciousness. Your authentic self is not a gift you are looking to receive. It is the only thing that you cannot lose or cannot be taken from you. It is you! Enjoy yourself.

IV

THE AUTHENTICALLY RESPONSIBLE SELF: THE GIFT OF CHOICE

Of all the gifts bestowed upon us as a species, as well as individuals, one gift stands out. The gift of choice or *free-will*; the ability to choose to do and be whatever we so desire. We can choose to live in the city, live in the country, live in an apartment, a mansion, a tent, or we can be homeless. We can drive any car we desire such as a Ford, Chevrolet, Buick, Mercedes, Range Rover, Ferrari, or we can choose to ride a motorcycle, catch the bus, a train or fly in a plane. The choice is up to us. We can also choose to live righteously or unrighteously; be miserable or happy. We can choose to create hell or heaven on earth. We can choose to have World War III (Armageddon), or we can choose peace. All being said, we have the power to create our own reality. The choice is ours.

Wars exist because of someone's choices. Evil exists because we've chosen it into our existence. Good or bad, the choice is ours to make. The question then becomes: If we realize that the root cause of all negativities is the consequence of choices, then why don't we make positive choices or right choices instead of wrong ones? One word is the answer to this question, and it is a simple word called *"blame"*. It is so easy to shift blame instead of taking responsibility for the outcomes of the choices we make.

Blame has become an entity within our society. It is a created "Devil" or "Demon" designed to take the responsibility off one's self and place it on an entity. It has taken the place of our internal responsibility. It is much easier to create an external culprit to blame, rather than take internal responsibility. These external foes have been created for blame to be placed on them; enemies such as demons, devils, Satan, external curses, black magic, sorcery, and witchcraft are illusive entities created to take the fault of the man in the mirror. Adam blames Eve for his shortcomings and Eve blamed the serpent. Even the external, unauthentic "God" is blamed for the demise of human progression.

The Choices You Make Come with the Consequences that You must Learn to Live With and not Blame

The responsibility of choice is a gift given to everyone. We should be careful and choose to be responsible and take ownership of this precious gift. The choices you make come with consequences that you must learn to live with and not blame. What will you do when the government fails, or the church doors close, or our guardians die? What will you stand upon, trust, or look to? What will you choose to do? **Isaiah 30:21** says:

And thine ears shall hear a word behind thee, saying, this [is] the way, walk ye in it, when ye turn to the right hand, and when ye turn to the left.
-KJV

David says in Psalms 121:1-2:

I will lift up mine eyes unto the hills, from whence cometh my help.
My help cometh from the Lord, which made heaven and earth.
-KJV

"The Best Gift I Can Give Myself is My Authentic Self"

Throughout my childhood and teenage years, I remember being totally at the mercy of my parents, elders, guardians, and religious leaders. As I grew older, many of them transitioned leaving me feeling diminished. It was during this expedition that I truly discovered that my identity was not dependent upon others, but myself. I have learned and am learning to create my own reality, and that the best gift I can give myself is my authentic self. Being true to yourself is the first step in making good choices and taking responsibility for those choices.

Some choices we make are not necessarily bad or good, they are merely learning experiences. My grandmother was the matriarch of the family. She always held everything together and seemed to have all the answers for everyone, no matter what problems or challenges we encountered. In a sense, we did not have to think for ourselves, because we depended on her to fix all our problems and situations. Then, she died suddenly at the age of 45 from a brain aneurysm. What were we going to do then?

During that time, I was in junior high school. I was the oldest grandchild. My mother had me at a young age, so I was close in age to several of my aunts and uncles. However, her passing changed our lives forever, because we all had to adopt a sense of responsibility that we did not have before she passed. This was a learning experience for all of us. We had to learn to make choices on our own and most of all, accept responsibility for our choices.

Because of my grandmother's sudden shift from this earthly journey, I learned during my young years to become responsible. I had to help my mother with my younger siblings, and sometimes be the man of the house. The time I did spend with my grandmother taught me a lot of things, and blame was not one of them. She taught us if you did wrong to take responsibility.

> *I learned that unfavorable conditions are not challenges to weaken us, but to strengthen us and compel us to continue in a favorable path.*

Sometimes when we make decisions in our life, we are uncertain of the outcome. We feel that this decision is what is right for me, and that whatever happens just happens. It is often in making these types of decisions that we learn the most valuable lessons of responsibility. Just remember, you made the decision and it was your choice.

I married and had a child at a young age. I then had to be responsible for a whole family. I chose to get married, and I could not blame anyone or anything for any deficiencies. I learned that unfavorable conditions are not challenges to weaken us, but to strengthen and compel us to continue on a more favorable path. If the household lacked finances, it was my responsibility to fix it. I could not blame the world or anyone for what I did not have. I had to take responsibility and make it happen. Sometimes that was a harsh truth, but the truth nonetheless, and the only way to be free was to set myself free, taking responsibility and dealing with it.

The authentic self will always take responsibility for the choices it makes. Choices are decisions that will always lead to responsibility being held. Responsibility is being accountable. As long as things are going right, it is easy to take responsibility, However, when something goes wrong, or at least seems unfavorable, responsibility must find a culprit. This is when blame is placed instead of assuming responsibility. Blame does not fix the situation; it always makes it worse as well as delays the inevitable. This is when unnecessary enemies are created and often become a Frankenstein in our lives. These unauthentic creatures can sometimes be hard to destroy because no one wants to take responsibility.

Do not Blame Something or Someone Else for Jumping off of the cliff when you made the choice to jump

There is an old cliché that many people used to say: "The devil made me do it." Really? Who is the Devil and how did he make you jump off a cliff? Is it a man with red horns, or perhaps it is another person that you surmised as being the culprit? Do not blame something or someone else for jumping off the cliff when you made the choice to jump. No matter the pressure from the outside (or even in your mind) that gives you the unction to do something, you made the choice to respond the way you did. Therefore, you should bear the responsibility for it. You can try and evade it, but ultimately, it will find its way back home to you.

I remember losing some keys this once. Instead of admitting that I had put them somewhere and could not remember where I left them, I decided to play the blame game. I let my ego take control and put the responsibility for my losing the keys on someone else. My wife was the recipient of the blame that day. No matter what she said, I would not admit that I lost them. Instead, I was certain she had moved them. She began to tell me to calm down, back track my steps and it would come to me. Well, I did that and a little while later, I found them in the freezer. I had to humble myself and apologize. I said that to say, "stop playing the blame game". Learn to take responsibility, then correct and learn from your mistakes. Blame no one and you will soon realize when you do not provide blame with a host, it will disappear. Don't even blame yourself, rather simply always be responsible. It is your choice.

V

TRUE RESPECT, REVERENCE AND UNITY

> *Everyone deserves equal respect no matter their culture, social standing or economic status.*

In such a society as ours today, it becomes so easy to look down on or judge someone else. This prejudgment often exacted because of a culture, monetary assets, neighborhood, place or position of employment, education and many other social and economic statuses. No matter who we are or what we have, it does not give us the right to judge others who may have less or are just simply different from us. Just because I like and can afford to eat steak everyday does not make me greater or superior to a person who eats chicken every day, be it by choice or circumstance. Different cultures, beliefs and values don't give us the privilege to disrespect one another.

We can have respect one for another even through our disparities, because most often our differences are just a matter of opinion or options that we personally choose. Everyone deserves equal respect no matter their culture, social standing or economic status. Simply put, respect yourself by respecting others. Treat others the way you would like to be treated.

From the moment we are born, we are given everything needed to survive in this life. As humans, we all are conceived in a womb that is perfectly made for us as an embryo to grow into a fetus. After birth we have food that nature provides in our mother's breasts or otherwise if the mother prefers not to breast feed. We have a body that is the very temple of God. We have a soul that is directly connected to, and very much a part of the universal soul [*God*]. We live in a world of nature that is wonderfully created. All we have to do is live in it and enjoy its existence and each other.

When we respect others, we respect ourselves.

One important actuality is that many of our mistakes come when we disrespect others and their right to choose their own decisions and responsibility. Many countries are respected and valued in the eyes of other countries, while other countries are not. Some families are perceived as prominent and respectable, while others are seen as beneath them. One race may be seen as superior, and all others subhuman. Many religions, holidays, cultures, banners, genders, doctrines are reputable and respected, but there seems to be a great divide and lack of respect in each of them. When we respect others, we respect ourselves.

Everyone has their own given right to govern their lives in the way in which they choose to do so. Often people use the name of God in vain to condemn others. This prejudice characteristic and personality is found in many religions, governments, nations, deities, and doctrines. This is indeed disrespectful. It is the direct result of an egotistical, narcissistic, selfish, condescending nature (the ego). Wow! Is not that the man in the mirror?

Your true soul has reverence for everyone and everything because everyone and everything has value even when they do not realize it. To think otherwise is to devalue yourself and the creator. Remember the scripture in **Luke 6:31 that says**

"And as ye would that men should do to you, do ye also to them likewise."

-KJV

It is (like) a karma effect. What you do to others will be done to you. It is very tempting to disrespect those that disrespect you, and it takes a presence of discipline not to do it. When someone disrespects another, the disrespectful person generally has some type of difficulty in that moment and uses blame as a scapegoat. Vengeance belongs to karma (reaping and sowing), and nothing, absolutely nothing, escapes its law. God is not waiting to judge you; karma (your own actions) judges you. An angry personality will find it quite easy to disrespect external entities. The angry personalities will often begin to dehumanize others by name-calling. For example, it is difficult to condemn a human being, but much easier to condemn a witch or a demon.

> *The seed of disrespect can be so strong that it influences the next generation to create the same karma as the generation before it, and sometimes even the children's children.*

There is a difference between a person being angry and an angry personality. An angry personality responds to all challenges of life with anger. An individual that is angry, yet respects life, will not lash out to harm others. The seed of disrespect can be so strong that it influences the next generation to create [sow] the same karma as the generation before it, and sometimes even the children's children. They cannot reap or sow your karma, but they can be influenced to keep it going by creating their own. This is called a generational curse, which is not broken until a generation chooses not to create the same karma. The scripture speaks of this in **Exodus 34:7**.

Keeping mercy for thousands, forgiving iniquity and transgression and sin, and that will by no means clear the guilty, visiting the iniquity of the fathers upon the children, and upon the children's children, unto the third and to the fourth generation.
-KJV

A malediction (curse) is illusive on its own. However, if you yield yourself to it and empower it, it will manifest the illusion of power over you. Once you yield and allow it to have power, you will then begin to look for external power (such as trinkets, rituals, ceremonies, exorcists, priests, etc.) to set you free. All of these external things only bring the illusion of freedom. All of that is to say, implying a curse upon someone is one of the most disrespectful ways a person can have about them. This low frequency of thinking and practicing is egotistical. If you are a truly respectful person, you would not resort to such.

What is in great demand now are people that respect each other and create an alliance of unity.

All fighting of people, and nations are the result of disrespect. Disrespectful personalities view life as cheap and without value. The respectful personality is in alignment with its soul. The soul has no respect of person. Meaning everyone is equal, though simply different (particularly on the outside, or in front of the veil). Muslim, Christians, and Jews can have harmony if they choose to. The division is often caused by disrespect. What I mean by harmony is that we can all disagree in some type of way yet respect each other through disagreeing.

Disrespect will cause a neighbor to throw away food before giving it to someone starving. Disrespect will cause you to look upon others as prey or competition and say, "it's a dog-eat-dog world" or "may the best man win". To live, the disrespectful will destroy others, thinking that everyone thinks as they do. They live to take and never give back. When we judge some as inferior and the others superior, we have omitted respect. What is in great demand now are people that respect each other and create an alliance of unity.

The unity of the human species is the origin of our existence. There is one type of human body, one human spirit and one human soul. God created only one human blueprint, called Adam. We are all Adam. Your authentic self is always striving for the moment when nothing else exist except respect for all. That will be heaven on earth; the kingdom. Respect is not something that is just wished for, we must make it happen as Jesus says in **Matthew 5:3-12**.

> *³Blessed are the poor in spirit: for theirs is the kingdom of heaven.*
> *⁴ Blessed are they that mourn: for they shall be comforted.*

> *⁵ Blessed are the meek: for they shall inherit the earth.*
> *⁶ Blessed are they which do hunger and thirst after righteousness: for they shall be filled.*
> *⁷ Blessed are the merciful: for they shall obtain mercy.*
> *⁸ Blessed are the pure in heart: for they shall see God.*
> *⁹ Blessed are the peacemakers: for they shall be called the children of God.*
> *¹⁰ Blessed are they which are persecuted for righteousness' sake: for theirs is the kingdom of heaven.*
> *¹¹ Blessed are ye, when men shall revile you, and persecute you, and shall say all manner of evil against you falsely, for my sake.*
> *¹² Rejoice, and be exceeding glad: for great is your reward in heaven: for so persecuted they the prophets which were before you.*
> *-KJV*

Take note of these scriptures as Jesus speaks. Authentic blessings come from the blueprint you create for them. For example, *"Blessed are the merciful, for they shall obtain mercy."* This scripture lets us know that mercy comes as a gift to yourself from yourself. Friends do not come by coincidence. If we want friends, we must show ourselves friendly. Our respect and kindness produce friends, and our disrespect produces enemies.

The path to your soul is knowing your heart. Others look at your outer appearance, but God sees your heart. Therefore, see your authentic self as only you can. When you find your authentic self (which is your Being), you have found God. There is no God more intimate than that. The reason why the search for God is still so intense is because the search is external. Not only do we need a respectful personality, but we also need a personality of reverence.

The difference between respect and reverence is respect is a response to qualities that we admire. Reverence is a oneness perception. It applies to a higher self that is not based on a judgement. To reverence God is to reverence all of creation, all of nature. Your authentic self is sacred. To live with reverence is the concept of "The way you treat people is the way you treat God".

It is human nature to live with reverence. Without it, the world would be a lonely, empty, and cruel place. It would be hell on earth. Reverence allows us to touch the soul of God. All things become one. Unity and harmony are in all things with a personality of reverence. Everyone and everything are respected. Reverence allows non-judgmental justices. It is the justice of God. Those who punish and harm others are not in touch with their soul. They are in touch with their personality's ego which lacks reverence. The personality of reverence beholds God [divinity] in all things and gives it honor [reverence].

Reverence also transforms the five sensory personalities into an extra or multi- sensory personality, which allows us and others to become individually and collectively the temple of God – natures intelligence. The extra sensory personality can discern our other body, the non-physical body. **2 Corinthians 5:1** says:

For we know that if our earthly house of this tabernacle were dissolved, we have a building of God, and house not made with hands, eternal in the heavens.
-KJV

We can live a life of reverence and respect while experiencing the blissfulness of life, or we can live a life without reverence and experience emptiness. To live each day with reverence and respect is to live the life of your authentic self.

VI

BREAKING THE CYCLE OF ILLUSION: LIVING IN THE NEWLY DISCOVERED CYCLE OF TRUTH

> *Christ is the God part of your TRUE BEING. Your True Being cannot leave Christ, and Christ cannot leave Your True Being.*

To live a complete and fulfilling existence in this [physical] world, we must find, exist, and live from the authentic consciousness and heart of self. Without consciousness, we as a species could not decide our fate, make decisions, or experience any of our five senses. Without consciousness we could not comprehend the intuition of our extra sensory selves. Consciousness allows us to obtain the intellect collected by our five sensory personalities. It also allows us to discuss and comprehend the messages of the nonphysical guides and teachers, which are sometimes called angels, ancestors, master teachers, etc. Consciousness allows us to communicate and relate to our being. It allows us to behold the Christ within ourselves. Christ is in everyone, but everyone does not discern and relate with it. Christ is the God part of your true being. Your True Being cannot leave Christ, and Christ cannot leave your True Being.

Philippians 1:21

²¹ For to me to live is Christ, and to die is gain.

-KJV

Colossians 1

²⁷ To whom God would make known what is the riches of the glory of this mystery among the Gentiles; which is Christ in you, the hope of glory:

-KJV

Christ is the part of God that lives in all humans. There is a Holy Spirit in everyone. However, it is often hidden by veils of blindness [ignorance], and that is why many never come to the knowledge of it or experience it. Many depend on external Christs, false Christs or something foreign as a guide. The Holy Spirit within you is yours personally. It relates with your thoughts, emotions, and behavior. It has your *shape [form]*. It is one with your authentic self. It is your authentic self! It is what connects you and I to the God family. It has nothing to do with religion, denomination, race, nationality, or gender. It has nothing to do with the ego [fleshly perception] period. It is the very essence of God.

Can you imagine if people would look inside themselves and really realize the glory of God and Its very Being living inside them? Wow!! We would have and see a different world. People would not want to hurt or kill one another. The cease fire in individuals would become the order of the day. What a beautiful world! However, when people defy the truth and live-in illusions, you can expect just about anything to happen. When people are unconscious, they take on the works of the flesh [ego] and live-in darkness.

The Holy Spirit (Ghost) cannot be bought. It is the heritage of every human being past, present and future

The spirit of God is that Light of truth that brings us into existence. It is a gift given by the one true God. The Holy Spirit (Ghost) cannot be bought. It is the heritage of every human being past, present and future, but it requires consciousness to discern and relate to it. The Holy spirit is discerned by the intuition of the multi-sensory consciousness. *Your* Holy Spirit is your consciousness and awareness of your non-physical being. Before you were a conscious physical being, you were a non-physical being with a high form of consciousness that is not perceived by the physical consciousness.

Learn to Truly Breathe and enjoy the Pause between each breath

Genesis 2:7
7 And the Lord God formed man of the dust of the ground and breathed into his nostrils the breath of life; and man became a living soul.
-KJV

Our non-physical being (Holy Spirit) was in existence before we arrived at existence. It will exist even when our physical journey is over. When we surrender to that truth, we enter heaven. We are not waiting for the physical journey to be over for this to occur, rather we can and should embrace it now. We do not live waiting for what is on the other side, rather live experiencing the other side [heaven] on this side [earth]. It may sound a little deep and awkward to some, but this is what accepting the spirit of God is all about.

On this journey we experience the breath of life. In between each breath is a pause. When we enter that place, it is there that we can find peace to escape the bitterness of egotistical thoughts and powers. In other words, learn to truly breathe and enjoy the pause between each breath. That is true meditation and prayer, and it manifests the depths of our desires and thoughts during our journey on this earth.

> *Be in the Moment. Escape Fear and Enjoy the Ride*

I have often heard people say that everything will be all right when we get to heaven. That is true to some extent, however they are referring to the afterlife. Why not experience heaven on this journey? We know that when we shed this physical body we will be at rest, but why do we have to wait (physically die) to get to the other side and experience God? You only live THIS journey once. When we shed this earthen vessel, this life's journey is over. So why not enjoy heaven now? Be in the moment! Escape fear and enjoy the ride.

> *Fear is the foundation of many missed opportunities we have on this journey.*

II Timothy 1:7
For God hath not given us the spirit of fear; but of power, and of love, and of a sound mind.
-KJV

Notice the scripture says the "spirit" of fear as opposed to just fear. Those very words let us know that fear must have company to become powerful. Fear comes in many faces and is very illusive. Fear is the foundation of many missed opportunities we have on this journey. Fear will literally cause us to stop in our tracks and become stuck.

Fear is made up of thought. Just as there is a space between our inhale and exhale, there is space between our thoughts of fear. Prayer and meditation allow us to notice that space, and it is then that we can allow our thought of fear to become a thought of confidence. It is then we can use that space to have another thought and that thought will not be a thought of fear, but rather a presence of calmness. Always remember you can control your thoughts and use that space given to do it.

> **There are many miracles missed during our moment (journey of life) because of fear.**

I remember being in the room with my wife when she was in labor with our second child. I was fearful about seeing my child being born. As a matter of fact, I was fearful of seeing anything of that nature. I kept telling myself it was going to be okay, yet I was nervous and fearful. There was a nurse who discerned my nervousness. She told me to take a deep breath, and know, it is going to be alright. It was then I noticed the space in between my breaths that allowed me to gather my composure to change the way I was thinking. Had I continued in fear, I would have missed witnessing the miracle of my child's birth. There are many miracles missed during our moment [journey of life] because of fear. Do not let fear take control of your journey, rather, take control of your fears, and experience life with no regrets.

VII

THE TRUTH

The type of truth you receive through your intuition is your personal truth. You should not force your personal truth onto someone else, and no one should force their personal truth onto you. You should simply share your newfound truth, and let others' personal conscious guide them to and through their own personal experience.

John 8:32

And ye shall know the truth, and the truth shall make you free.
-KJV

Notice the words ye and you in the aforementioned scripture. Ye is collective and applies to the general population, while you applies specifically to you as an individual. There is a truth that applies to all of us, yet it is through the general truth that we find that personal connection of truth. Sometimes others will attempt to impose their personal truth upon you to promote and implant fear within you. This is especially true when someone is trying to control you or want you to come to their side of the table. If you yield, it is the birth of a personality of fear and bondage that is not aligned with your soul.

For instance, spiritual bullies will tell you that you are to live your life as they do (and say), or you are out of the will of God. You must learn to not be afraid of spiritual bullies. God is not a revelation given to you from without [externally]. God is revealed from within your authentic self. You are the only one that can give personal truth to you. Your reality is whatever your authentic self says it is. Do not be afraid to create and accept your own reality. It is that personal truth that makes you free.

I often call to mind the movie about Harriet Tubman and her journey from bondage. It was during one of her travels that she was having a conversation with a man who was helping her during her expedition. He was telling her that God allowed her to be free and she should be still and accept the freedom given to her and not try to go back and get others at the moment. Harriet responded by telling him that she was aware of God being there. However, it was her feet that did the running to get her out of bondage. What she wanted him to know was she was aware of God and where God was. She also wanted him to know that her content [flesh] participated in her freedom. She was conscious of the energy that was flowing from her non-content (Being) to her content (flesh) that brought her freedom.

Genesis 2:19 says:

And out of the ground the Lord God formed every beast of the field, and every fowl of the air; and brought them unto Adam to see what he would call them: and whatsoever Adam called every living creature, that was the name thereof.
-KJV

Adam was able to identify with animals and birds by names that he created. He participated in the reality of the Garden of Eden [his paradise]. God allowed him to do this, and he was aware of his participation in the creation. When we know who we are, we become aware of the God within. When we lose this awareness, we don't know ourselves. We lose truth.

When you are living a lie, your personality, which is lost, is seeking its way back to your Being. All of your personalities desire to serve your Being, even the ones that are negative. It is the ego [content] that gets in our way of identifying our Being, and therefore, causes us to do things that are undesirable. The universe and all of nature serves God. When you live as your authentic self, all the energy of the universe is at your service, and you are its light.

> *Matthew 5:14-16*
> *¹⁴ Ye are the light of the world. A city that is set on an hill cannot be hid.*
> *¹⁵ Neither do men light a candle, and put it under a bushel, but on a candlestick; and it giveth light unto all that are in the house.*
> *¹⁶ Let your light so shine before men, that they may see your good works, and glorify your Father which is in heaven.*
> *-KJV*

Not only do you serve God, but God serves you. Everything that we need is already given to us by the laws of nature. The needs met by these laws are called authentic needs. Those things often go unappreciated and taken for granted. So often we are unthankful for needs that are not met according to our time. Sometimes it is not that our needs are not being met, it is that we think they are authentic needs when they are in fact unauthentic needs. In other words, it is a want and not a true need. It is a fact that God does not supply [unauthentic] needs of our personalities, but according to scripture, He supplies all [authentic] needs of the individual He created.

> *Philippians 4:19*
> *¹⁹ But my God shall supply all your need according to his riches in glory by Christ Jesus.*
> *-KJV*

Personal truth will never cancel out, rather fulfill, general [impersonal] truth. This type of truth belongs to everyone; to all. General truth is the laws of nature that applies to everyone, such as karma [reaping ad sowing]. Intuition is something that must be desired and sought after. Intuition delivers truth. We receive it by:

Asking= receive (focus your mind)
Seeking= find (find the truth)
Knocking= door opened. (walk in truth)

Matthew 7:7-8
7 Ask, and it shall be given you; seek, and ye shall find; knock, and it shall be opened unto you:
8 For every one that asketh receiveth; and he that seeketh findeth; and to him that knocketh it shall be opened.
-KJV

If you do not ask, seek and knock, you will remain without truth. People's hindrance is their own fear [created personality] of truth. They think truth can cause them harm, which truth is incapable of doing. When truth is absent, the authentic self has not been revealed, and you are prisoner to the dominant unauthentic self. The only thing that can free you is truth. As mentioned before,

John 8:32
32 And ye shall know the truth, and the truth shall make you free.
-KJV

Again, NOTHING EXTERNAL CAN FACILITATE YOUR FREEDOM! If it does, it is not authentic freedom, only the illusion of freedom. General truths are the assistance and guidance provided to everyone. They are the laws of God given to relate and assist all human beings as nonphysical guides, often called angels. The authentic self knows we are never alone. Truth is always present. Truth reveals love [God] through intuition. Everything else is an illusion designed to reveal what is not authentic.

Illusions are real, but the objects they reveal are not.

You must remove the veil to discover what is behind it. Illusions are real, but the objects they reveal are not. Illusions are not necessarily a bad thing for humans. In fact, they reveal what is authentic by revealing what is not authentic. Illusion reveals truth by removing the veil of the lie.

Illusions are only in this physical content. In other words, we see reality on the other side of the illusion. When we die, the illusions die also, because it is not of the eternal soul. Illusion allows us to change [repent] from the unauthentic into the authentic. It allows us to heal and become whole. Illusions will reveal the lie without it affecting you. However, once you enter or accept fear, the object of the illusion becomes real to you. Consequentially, something unreal is controlling your thoughts, emotions, and behavior. The object of illusion receives its power from you; and as you gave it power, only you can take the power away.

Negative personalities are filled with illusion: jealousy, greed, bullying, manipulation, violence, ridicule, judgement. These are all offerings of fear. All of them are illusions, including fear derived from our thoughts. When your intuitive nature hears the voice of these illusions and transforms them into truth, torment is created. Until the negative personality finds its soul, therefore, finding truth (the authentic self), it will continue in distress. In the authentic self, there is no torment, just love. This is where heaven [paradise] abides. Our desire is to remove the veil of illusion that is causing us torment, so we may abide in heavenly places.

In an earlier chapter concerning consciousness, we mentioned the importance of being aware of each moment of thought. The unconscious personality is not aware of its thoughts. It is veiled by blindness. This veil must be destroyed.

Matthew 27:51

[51] And, behold, the veil of the temple was rent in twain from the top to the bottom; and the earth did quake, and the rocks rent;

-KJV

RELIGION

Your authentic self is beyond religion. It not only searches for God, but it identifies God and experiences God through essence. Many things taught today in religion are blind spots.

These blind spots are referred to as the religious personality, which is controlled from the outside. Truth will never be obtained when the personality is ruled by external forces, even if it is in religion. Religion keeps groups united, but they are prejudice in doctrine. Prejudice was the problem that Jesus had with their (then) present-day beliefs.

Even today, many religions are fighting for [external] power over people, and many will sing and preach the name of the Lord in vain to get it. We must not think that a religious God of a particular religion is the one and only true God, because God is not religious or prejudice. God is God! Our job to each other is to encourage, enlighten and bring people to God within themselves, not condemn them. Jesus was not prejudice, and was rejected, excommunicated, condemned, and crucified for not being prejudice. Jesus introduced us through His teachings to a new way of worship, called, spirit and truth. We can now experience the essence of God in and through us.

Because of the veil of the religious personality, many are unable to see the negative karma that they are creating for themselves. Illusion reveals what is wrong to you before you create a negative personality and negative karma along with it. Negative karma is easy to produce when the person is unaware of their thoughts at that moment; and therefore, unaware of the karma they created. Remember, all karma delivers truth back to you, whether positive or negative. This truth provides light for your next choice and new karma, as the old karma dies.

Every human being is constantly creating new karma. These actions define our effect from cause. We have the ability to heal ourselves or remain diseased and stagnant. This is emotionally, socially, spiritually, as well as physically. Oddly, it is controversial to notion that God has nonjudgmental justice called karma to bring fairness to all *(reaping and sowing - Galatians 6:7 -KJV)*. However, no one can say truthfully that God has grace and mercy on some, but not others. Grace and mercy are gifts that we give to ourselves through the karma we create. If we are merciful, mercy will return to us. If we are friendly, we will have friends. If we forgive others, then we are forgiven. We must remember that we create our fate.

Ultimately and truthfully, all authentic needs are given to your soul. Nothing else is needed. Remember, not only do you serve God, but God serves you. He meets the needs of your authenticity. All unauthentic needs are desired to satisfy our negative personalities. Positive personalities live off the authentic needs of the soul, wanting nothing, as David addressed in

Psalms 23
¹The Lord is my shepherd; I shall not want.
-KJV

The [true] authentic self has all the essentials; therefore, we should be truly thankful to God the Father. Once you begin to stop focusing on unauthentic needs and putting them at the forefront of your life, you will become more compassionate towards the needs of others. When you find yourself in this place of compassion for others, you are your most powerful self.

Luke 22:27

²⁷ For whether is greater, he that sitteth at meat, or he that serveth? is not he that sitteth at meat? but I am among you as he that serveth.

-KJV

VIII

BECOMING AUTHENTICALLY ME: "THE PRACTITIONER"

Your life is but a moment. It is the period between sunrise [when you were born into this world] and sunset [when you die or leave this earthy journey].

When you come to discover your true and authentic self, you begin to look at life differently and most of all you begin to act or behave differently. You become a "practitioner" of all the things that you have learned and all the information you have attained over the years. Most importantly, when you have truly awakened, your eyes become crystal clear. All the floaters disappear.

Your life is but a moment. It is the period between sunrise [when you are born into this world] and sunset [when you die or leave this earthly journey]. You cannot live this life [moment] on the other side of sunset. You live this life NOW! So, once you awaken to your true self, you anxiously anticipate each day to exercise and put into practice your newly found experience of freedom.

The rest of this chapter will outline some of the enlighten frames of life that you begin to look at through a new set of lenses. It is not that you have not known some of these things, it is that you see them in a clearer, more defined picture. This makes the practice even the more encouraging and eventful as each day goes by. Remember this is just a few of the many frames you will experience in your journey called life.

LOVE AND FORGIVENESS

True love is internal freedom. It has no boundaries. Its energy is everlasting. To love unconditionally and freely most often requires forgiveness, which is the emission of something you have done, or something done to you. There are times when we say we have forgiven someone, but we are still holding on to what they did to us. When you want others to be constantly reminded that you forgave them, it is not authentic forgiveness.

Unauthentic forgiveness is when you forgive someone to gain power over them. It is a way to receive external power over others. You hold it over their head. This type of forgiveness manipulates others. This is the work of the unauthentic self [ego], an act of egotism and not true unconditional love and forgiveness. Authentic forgiveness means that all dead weights of your experiences are left behind. True forgiveness means looking at life without the pain from the past harmful experiences of others or yourself. Continuing to cast blame and wanting someone else to be accountable for your pain and sorrow is the sign of an unforgiving heart, and not a loving heart.

Martin Luther King said that love isn't love if it is not being given away. Love is the heartfelt commitment or connection to something or someone that flows from the center of your heart, which is your true and authentic self. To experience true love and forgiveness is to experience the perfectly free relationship. Forgiveness is not only forgiving others, but it is also forgiving yourself through others. It sets both you and the other person free. From this relationship, lessons have been learned, connections made, and you can move in forward progression.

Forgiving and loving seems easier said than done. When you have been caused pain by the actions of others, it can be quite difficult to forgive. Coming to the realization that a person is being used by an unauthentic personality to cause harm or maybe even death can be quite difficult to digest. In fact, more than often retaliation comes to mind before love and forgiveness. I can use many examples; some awfully hard to fathom and some relatively easy. The bottom-line question is, can you truly forgive, and do you have true love for all? Now, this does not at all mean to forget everything done to you. It simply means to move past those barriers that cut off or block your connection to freedom. When you find your authentic self, you find true love and that love is God. Sounds simple, huh?

I john 4:8 says:
He that loveth not knoweth not God; for God is love.
-KJV

I Corinthians 13 quotes:
¹Though I speak with the tongues of men and of angels, and have not charity, I am become as sounding brass, or a tinkling cymbal.
² And though I have the gift of prophecy, and understand all mysteries, and all knowledge; and though I have all faith, so that I could remove mountains, and have not charity, I am nothing.
³ And though I bestow all my goods to feed the poor, and though I give my body to be burned, and have not charity, it profiteth me nothing.

⁴ Charity suffereth long, and is kind; charity envieth not; charity vaunteth not itself, is not puffed up,
⁵ Doth not behave itself unseemly, seeketh not her own, is not easily provoked, thinketh no evil;
⁶ Rejoiceth not in iniquity, but rejoiceth in the truth;
⁷ Beareth all things, believeth all things, hopeth all things, endureth all things.
⁸ Charity never faileth: but whether there be prophecies, they shall fail; whether there be tongues, they shall cease; whether there be knowledge, it shall vanish away.
-KJV

There is nothing greater than love. Love is the king attribute of the authentic self. It is the essence of God. We must possess the personalities of love and forgiveness. Without it, we are not free. We must love ourselves and others and we must learn to forgive ourselves and others. We must show this in our practice of living and not just words coming from our mouth. **James 1:22-24** tells us:

²² But be ye doers of the word, and not hearers only, deceiving your own selves.
²³ For if any be a hearer of the word, and not a doer, he is like unto a man beholding his natural face in a glass:
²⁴ For he beholdeth himself, and goeth his way, and straightway forgetteth what manner of man he was.
-KJV

CREATIVITY

Everyone has a different reality. Do not be afraid to do it your way. Have your own style, your own brand, your own label. It is alright to sing someone else's song sometimes but do it your way. Put your persona spin on it. Be creative, become an original and release the imagination in your authentic self.

Our ancestors in scripture gave us of their personal experiences and relationship with God. While we read, quote, and practice their teachings, the reality is that their experiences become our experiences but in our own way. For instance, Paul may have said "If God be for us, who can be against us?", but he should not be the only one who says that. This scripture should be just as much ours as it is his, because its true for us as well. Make that scripture yours. The true authentic self does not imitate, but rather brings into existence its own truth.

Being creative means to have or show the ability to make [create] new things or think new ideas. Use your ability to create. It is your God given ability that is shared by God. Do not settle for imitations, use your imagination, and work it. Let it do its thing. You were created to be unique. There is only one you. It is alright to desire and mark the traits and characteristics of others, but have those desires and traits lived through you being you. Your creativity is your freedom to create your paradise [home/world]. Wear your colors and choose your accessories. Decorate to fulfill your own imagination. You cannot have ingenious ideas if you do not use your imagination. Be innovative, be original, be authentic. Allow your mind to dream to disconnect you from status quo. An ingenious idea is an idea or vision that has not happened yet. It is something that you have desired, and you should have fun doing it.

Before I decided to start a homeschooling program at our church, I was teaching at another school. I was grateful for the opportunity given to me by a lady who had her own school, envisioned by her. It was through that opportunity that encouraged me to have and start my own homeschool. I envisioned servicing children from first through the twelfth grade, providing an opportunity for them to enter college.

Being a teacher, you have to create different ways to impart learning in the classroom, especially in a non-traditional setting. One method [creativity] I used was letting the more advanced children teach the unadvanced children during some of our social activities and classes. I did not know if it would work. However, it turned out to be a charm, especially with the boys. Not only did it help them to learn from one another, but it enabled them to work together as a team.

Out of the five years we had the school, we had five high school graduates, and every one of them was able to get enrolled into college. Once enrolled, the rest was up to them. Moreover,

I am thankful that we fulfilled the vision of getting them to college. Wherever you place your attention will manifest itself. That is the law [power] of creativity [creation].

> *The authentic self always reaches satisfaction. It is the unauthentic self that is never satisfied and unfulfilled.*

AFFIRMATION

Affirmation is the intention of the authentic self [soul]. It is not an external experience, rather it is an internal experience. Affirmation is not asking an external entity for something. It is the alignment of all your personalities with your soul. You speak to your soul, as your soul is always in harmony with the universe [God]. We should live our lives in touch, aware and in harmony with our soul. When this happens, we are in constant affirmation. We are affirming [praying] without ceasing, transforming our personality into our authentic self and never wanting [whole].

Through affirmation, every intention is acquired, and all authentic petitions are answered. Affirmation is not wishful or guesswork to a petition, it is the petition. All your authentic needs are already accessible. Affirmation is the connection to review them consciously and thankfully.

1 Thessalonians 5:18:
In every thing give thanks: for this is the will of God in Christ Jesus concerning you.
-KJV

EVOLUTION

The authentic self always reaches fulfillment. It is the unauthentic self that is never satisfied and unfulfilled. It is through affirmation that all things are brought into existence and manifested.

> *Allow Yourself to experience growth of your new-found Being (Your Authentic Self) EVOLVE!*

One of the biggest roadblocks to individualization and self-realization is people not being able to evolve. Regardless of how good you think you are today; tomorrow should bring about some improvement. You should never stop learning or developing. Continue to grow daily. Stretch your intellect. Do not have that *"know it all"* personality. Stop being afraid of yourself. Allow yourself to experience growth of your new-found being [Your Authentic Self]. EVOLVE!

While evolving is easier said than done, when you discover your authentic self, you will become in harmony with evolution and roll with it. You will become inquisitive as to what you have been missing. You simply must not be afraid of it. At first you might think that you have seen a ghost, but don't run, it is only your true self. You will be ever so happy to discover what is behind that veil.

Growing up, I spent a lot of time alone in the woods, taking long walks and using my imagination to take me outside of myself. This was not just my normal natural surroundings, but it included my inner self. I always thought I was a stranger to myself trying to find my real identity. I had a hard time sleeping in the dark. I was afraid to close my eyes because I did not know what I was going to see. One day I decided that I was not going to afraid anymore, and whatever I saw when I closed my eyes, I was going to embrace it. Guess what? The only thing I saw was myself. I discovered in this moment that I had conquered fear. All I ever saw was just me. I had been stressing myself out over something that I imagined had a desire to harm me.

Learn to relax, destress and refine yourself daily. Take care of your mind and your body. Seek methods that work for you as an individual. Position yourself for the next wave in your life. Avoid becoming bored and stale. Be self-motivated and keep the fire burning. However, do not take on more than you can handle. Focus on cultivating your life doing the necessary work one moment at a time. Make your nice personalities nicer. Get the counseling you need, attend conferences, attend seminars, talk to people and hear their stories and experiences. Keep up with the times. Get involved in programs to minister to the hurting, the needy and the outcasts. Remember faith without works is dead. Enjoy both the works and the harvest. Believe in yourself. What you could not do yesterday, know that you can do it today.

RESILIENCE

Be Resilient. The authentic self cannot be defeated because it has no enemies. Resilience is the ability to stay strong, healthy, or successful again and again after experiencing adversity. Being able to return to an original shape after being pulled, stretched, pressed and bent is an art. It is an art that sometimes requires a great deal of spiritual, moral, and emotional substance. Adversity is a part of the human life that we will experience on this journey, but with resilience we are overcomers.

I John 4: 4
⁴Ye are of God, little children, and have overcome them: because greater is he that is in you, than he that is in the world.
-KJV

Your authentic self never quits. **II Corinthians 4:8** says:

We are troubled on every side, yet not distressed; we are perplexed, but not in despair;
-KJV

Keep hope alive! There will be so many voices that say you cannot, but those voices can be silenced by your authentic power. It is alright to take a rest, to recharge your battery and prepare to create more progress. Fredrick Douglass said, *"Where there is no struggle, there is not progress"*. What encouraging words. Make them your own. Weeping endures for a moment, then joy comes. After a woman travail in labor, deliverance comes with a gift and overwhelming joy.

James 1:2 says:
²My brethren, count it all joy when ye fall into divers temptations;
³ Knowing this, that the trying of your faith worketh patience.
-KJV

Patience will deliver all things. It completes you and gives you everything and you will not want for anything. Always remain open to the lessons to be learned. Every experience you encounter has a lesson, even the bad ones. Your loneliness, pain, distresses, disappointments, addictions and setbacks are all pathways to your awareness of what to change. Remember that all things work together for your good. These lessons are given by the guide and master of your soul, the very present help in your time of need. That is where your light of resilience comes from.

Your authentic self is never disconnected or without harmony with all authentic things. It is always in harmony and connected to the authentic guide, Master and Father. They all live within the authentic self. To know that we are not separate entities from the God within is what the joy of life is all about. We know this truth; we experience it through enlightenment.

ALIGNING YOURSELF WITH YOURSELF

Much of the process of discovering your true identity is being able to embrace truth and allow your current frame to align with your true frame. It is a part of the evolving process of the journey of discovering and becoming your authentic self. This chapter takes you to a place of becoming "The Practitioner", aligning yourself with yourself. This means to become one with your true authentic self. This is that truth that you have been trying to find during this expedition of life.

All along this voyage we have addressed the authentic and the unauthentic, the physical and non-physical existence. We have discovered consciousness and truth, and the responsibility and choices that come with it. We've established true respect and reverence, breaking the cycle of illusion and discovered hidden truths. Now we have arrived at this part of our destination that takes us into a world that is far beyond the veil. How did we get here?

After travelling here, we have truly discovered within ourselves the love, forgiveness and freedom relationship, and demolished those barriers that kept us bound. We now have clear access to all blessings in life. We have discovered our creative imagination within our true selves to design our paths to happiness and relentless freedom. We have experienced growth and the resilience that we were born with. We are here! Practitioners of who we really are, aligned with our true self.

Position Yourself Where Your Authentic Self Is

You have arrived at a place of internal fulfillment in which you are practicing and continue to progress. It is the place where you live from the inside and experience on the outside. Position yourself where your authentic self is. Your intuition will determine your position in the moment. Your position is your appointment. The universal authentic existence has already ordained your place before you were born into flesh.

Jeremiah 1:5 :
Before I formed thee in the belly I knew thee; and before thou camest forth out of the womb I sanctified thee, and I ordained thee a prophet unto the nations.
-KJV

IX

AUTHENTICALLY ME

Let your Authentic Life Shine and Live One Moment at A Time

We now have arrived at the true person in the mirror. The journey is not complete until your moment has expired, so continue to appreciate and enjoy the bliss of who you are in your moment. Let your authentic life shine and live one moment at a time within the moment of your journey. Love and live your life free of judgement and condemnation.

Romans 8:1
There is therefore now no condemnation to them which are in Christ Jesus, who walk not after the flesh, but after the Spirit.
-KJV

> *You are an eternal light and energy to be reflected upon everything in your space or purpose in the moment.*

Allow others to behold your authentic self. Your authentic self is your true light shining for all to see. Not only in the physical world, but also in the nonphysical world. You are visible to the past, present and future. Matthew 5:14 says that

> *Ye are the light of the world. A city that is set on an hill cannot be hid.*
> *-KJV*

So shine! **Matthew 5:16** says to
Let your light so shine before men, that they may see your good works, and glorify your Father which is in heaven.
-KJV

Your good works are those of your authentic self, which brings love, hope, peace, harmony, and sanity to others. You are an eternal light and energy to be reflected upon everything in your space and purpose in the moment. With every move you make, every step you take, every breath you breathe, every thought you think, know the universe [God] is doing it with you simultaneously. You are the embodiment and essence of God [Christ] in you.

Colossians 1:27:
To whom God would make known what is the riches of the glory of this mystery among the Gentiles; which is Christ in you, the hope of glory:
-KJV

Now that you can clearly see who, what, why, where and how you are, let it be known. Let it shine! As it [the light in you] shines, you become a beacon of the glory of what many call God. Not only does the sun give light and life, but it is also a magnet to the entire solar system. Your light is reflected on everything associated with you. Become that magnet of light. Do not take your light for granted. The sun is 93,000,000 miles away and still produces light and temperatures over 100 degrees on earth. The motivational force behind your light is love for everything in its presence. When your "Moment" is over [the time between sunrise and sunset], when you are no longer a physical human being, your light will shine forever in its authentic body of light, because you are and will forever be "authentically me". Again,

II Corinthians 5:1
For we know that if our earthly house of this tabernacle were dissolved, we have a building of God, an house not made with hands, eternal in the heavens.
-KJV

Get to know yourself and experience your moment. Always remember, your moment is the time between your sunrise [birth] and sunset [transition]. This is known as "The Journey". It is not the end; it is your moment. The authentic you has no end because it is not temporal.

Discover what is authentic and the unauthentic. Look beyond the mirror of your mind and find the real you behind the veil. Have a relationship with the God that is inside of you. Learn to get acquainted with the physical and the non-physical side of you, and allow them to harmonize. You will find that this experience is awesome! You will never want to lose you again once you awaken to your true self [consciousness].

Practice being authentically responsible for all your actions. Learn to talk to your thoughts. They will obey you. You are in control of you. Never forget! Experience truth, respect and unity during your journey. Do not focus on the ego [flesh] experience, but rather let your ego become subject to the true person inside of you which is the Holy Spirit.

> *Break the cycle of illusion.*
> *Escape fear and become the life of light.*

Become a practitioner of the Word. Break the cycle of illusion. Escape fear and become the life of light. Discover the new you and live in truth, becoming the practitioner. The Word of God or the Bible is no good in the book. It must come out of the book before it can make a difference. It must be lived. For so long, theory and concept were the order of the day. When you discover who you are, you discover life [God]. Discover truth and live it. Be truth.

> *Living the best of both worlds is authentically me.*

I am truly enjoying my journey right now. Living the best of both worlds is authentically me. Do not be afraid to be okay. Stop looking for darkness to find light. Everything can go well, and nothing has to be wrong for you to be okay in the moment. Live life and live it more abundantly.

I hope that this expedition has encouraged and enlightened you to look at what is inside of you, and not be afraid to embrace it. Let the sunshine in and become authentically me.

Peace and Blessings Upon You!

My next book "Beyond the Veil" is coming late 2022
Contact information
bobbyefelder@gmail.com
authenticallymebefelder.com
authenticallyme.covenant@gmail.com
Authentically Me (@OneAuthenticMe) / Twitter

Acknowledgements

First, I would like to personally thank Charity Greenfield for typing the first word and manuscript for this book. I sincerely appreciate your patience, will power and endurance for those many handwritten pages being made electronically available. It is not easy reading and understanding my handwriting. Again, "Thank You."

I would also like to thank my engineer, contributing editor, son and namesake, Bobby Felder II for coordinating and bringing this book to life. Without his expertise, hard work and resilience, this book would have not come to fruition.

Special thanks to my sons, Joshua Felder and Michiel Beasley for their monetary contributions towards the publishing of this book.

I acknowledge my friend and brother, P.D. Hester (known as the Prophet) for his listening ear, encouragement, support and non-judgement. He has been a friend indeed.

Additionally, I would like to thank Toosheyah (Mary Katherine) Chapman for her inspiration at a time I needed it most. Her enlightenment and encouragement have inspired me along my path, much more than she will ever know.

Lastly, my wife, Georgina for working with everyone, especially me throughout this journey. She was there from beginning to end making sure every intricate detail was absolute and unmitigated. She is a motivated spirit like none that I have ever known. She keeps going through all adversities. I love her and thank her for being the other half of my life.

www.ingramcontent.com/pod-product-compliance
Lightning Source LLC
Chambersburg PA
CBHW051457290426
44109CB00016B/1788